James M. Neil,
23, Glasgow Road,
Kilmarnock.

14·3·74.

POSTAGE STAMPS
MODERN HISTORY IN THE MAIL

With an introduction by Uberto Tosco

ORBIS BOOKS
LONDON

Contents

All the photographs in this volume are by Carlo Bevilacqua, with the exception of the following: plates 28, 29, 34, 42, 43, 46, 66, 68, 70, 72–4, 80, 81, 86, 92, 110, 124–6, 128 (Alain Grégoire); plates 5, 18, 19, 21 (Collection ancienne maison Théodore Champion); pages 10, 13, 14, and plates 38, 140 (Stanley Gibbons); 24 (Robson Lowe of London/ Michael Holford)

Translated from the Italian of Uberto Tosco

Printed in Italy by IGDA, Novara
SBN 0 85613 111 3

The last two decades have witnessed a marked resurgence of interest in stamp-collecting, following its sharp decline in popularity during the immediate post-war years. Popular interest has been reflected by the attention given to this pursuit by the daily press; indeed some newspapers allocate as much space to postage stamps and collecting as they do to radio and television.

Philately (from the Greek: *philos* (love); *ateleia* (tax-exemption), a reference to the postage stamp's special function in making a letter tax-free to the recipient) is much more than a simple hobby or pastime. It is neither a childish pursuit (although stamp-collecting is of absorbing interest to countless children) nor is it a somewhat bizarre passion for tracking down little slips of paper which were once used in the post, and are now reserved for the attention of dedicated specialists. Philately occupies a valuable and esteemed place in the broad field of education.

Stamp-collecting today follows several clearly defined paths. First, there is the general collection. This is concerned purely and simply with the random collection of every kind of stamp from every country and place, irrespective of shape, colour, size or value. Secondly, come the specialist collections. These tend to be limited to certain countries or historical periods, or concentrated on a special theme or aspect of postal communications, from the development of postage stamps and mail services, to methods of printing and design. And there are specialists who concentrate on searching for rare and unusual stamps, chiefly as a financial investment. Thirdly, there are the more glamorous, highly sophisticated and elaborate universal collections, constituting a unique ensemble of the various aspects of philately. Such collections are not only the best 'dressed' and organised, but also the most expensive, however rewarding they may ultimately prove for the speculator.

Whatever the different methods, objectives and motives of stamp collectors, the fact remains that philately suffers from a notable shortage of adequate and sufficiently comprehensive bibliographical information. There are, of course, a number of excellent general catalogues available, as well as informed magazines and periodicals, and specialist studies of different aspects and branches of philately. But these do not provide the sort of groundwork in philately that many collectors would like to acquire; in particular, a background to the development of postal services that can be consulted with profit, and without the fear of getting bogged down in detail.

This book aims, in a modest way, to satisfy this need. It sets out to provide a realistic outline for a satisfying collection, and a practical approach to achieving different goals in philately. At the same time, the possible financial rewards of judicious collecting are not ignored. Above all, however, it is concerned with demonstrating the links between developments in postal communications and outside historical events. Postal services have not only helped to increase the contact between different peoples and nations; they themselves reflect the impact of history and the influence of outstanding individuals – mainly through the character and appearance of postage stamps. A stamp collection is something more than merely a collection of national emblems and armorial bearings, portraits of kings and queens or picturesque engravings and representations. It is, in effect, a history, a pictorial record of the development of peoples, states and continents since the advent of the postage stamp.

We hope that this book will attract new enthusiasts to philately, and demonstrate, within limits, that stamps are something more than attractive coloured slips of paper or the official indication that the tax required by Caesar has in fact been rendered.

Uberto Tosco

A postmark used by the Republic of Venice during 1732–3. The letters stand for 'Posta De La Serenissima Signoria' (the Venetian Senate).

The postal service

It is difficult to imagine any kind of human society functioning without some sort of postal service, because one characteristic common to all people at all times is the need to communicate with one another and gain information. (Even Noah had to rely on the postal services of a dove and a raven to provide the Ark with information about the state of the Great Flood.) Human beings have always felt the urge – or the need – to travel, to explore the surface of the globe. Travelling men and women, traders, emigrants and adventurers have usually been under an equally strong compulsion to keep in touch with those they have left behind, to provide their compatriots with reports on their movements and experiences, as well as to keep abreast of events at home.

Every form of expedient has been adopted to maintain this vital contact. Nomads, caravans of merchants and traders, shepherds and slaves: these were the first couriers, and therefore the first effective postmen. At first, of course, these couriers brought their news by word of mouth. The ancient Egyptians, and later the Greeks and Romans, improved on this by transcribing messages on papyrus, parchment and thin tablets of clay. More often than not, these messages were concerned with military events, natural disasters, epidemics and other calamities. These dispatches were transported by every known form of conveyance, from camels, donkeys and horses to ships, carts and carriages.

Over the years, these embryonic postal systems became somewhat more elaborate. A series of halts was developed to facilitate the carriage of dispatches from one stage to the next. These were, literally, the 'post' at which couriers could leave or collect correspondence. If the post was originally a tree, then dispatches could be left in a hollow of the trunk. It was only a short step from that to fixing a coffer or box on poles, the forerunner of letter boxes and staging posts at which packets, parcels, goods and even people could be picked up and put down. It was only a matter of time before staging points of special importance were administered by a permanent staff, to become not only the initial post offices, but a focal point of the town centre.

The distance between staging posts became, in fact, the standard means of assessing the charges which it was up to the courier to levy. Although couriers were, for the most part, in the employ of the sender, they customarily received payment for the delivery from the recipient. The official seals or markings on the covers of correspondence, the forerunners of postage stamps, represented a receipt for tax paid to local authorities or governments as the toll for travelling through their territory.

Not surprisingly, the reliability of messengers was frequently in question. Couriers could choose from an almost infinite variety of excuses for delay, as there always were, or might always have been, accidents, hold-ups, breakdowns, and other obstructions to justify tardiness, or outright failure. Private citizens, but above all, the governments of cities, states and local authorities had every reason for wanting news as quickly as possible. It was essential for their well-being, and for the progress of public and private affairs. Steps had to be taken to guarantee the integrity of the couriers, and the delivery of mail in the shortest possible time.

Before the invention of the envelope it was the custom to write instructions to the courier on the outside of the messages being carried (plate 2). These instructions underscored the importance of the particular item of mail, and the need for speed. The Latin word for speed, *cito*, frequently appeared on the outside of the communication, its importance emphasised by repetition, *cito, cito!* Later, the inscription was further expanded to stress the urgency of speed by quadrupling the exhortation, often supplemented by additional instructions, *citissime! volante!* (Hurry up! Fly!) Sometimes a rudimentary drawing of a pitchfork was added, as a graphic reminder of the penalty awaiting laggards.

Today, collectors are paying increasing attention to this period, and there is continuous research and study into the origins of these pioneer postal services.

Facsimilies of postmarks used by Venetian post offices during the eighteenth century.

Paper-post and sealing wax

Little by little the courier mail became an indispensable public service. There were others besides the rich and powerful who wanted to communicate with distant parts, and towards the end of the sixteenth century correspondence could be sent, by anyone, virtually anywhere in Europe. All that was needed was sufficient money to pay dues, which were heavy enough, and the ability to write, which was rare enough. But there was always the possibility of using the services of a public letter-writer or a notary, officially qualified to draw up documents or witness transactions.

Early post offices, of course, had little in common with their modern counterparts. They were frequently crude buildings, shacks or hutments, and were distinguished by their characteristic trade sign flapping in the wind or painted on the wall. The post-horn, initially the distinguishing sign of the courier, had quickly been adopted as the trademark of the mail service, and was later to be painted on the sides of diligences (stage coaches) carrying the post. Post offices were the obvious focal points for town gossip and curiosity. They attracted the anxious and the inquisitive, a constant stream of humanity hoping to glean snatches of advance information, or eavesdrop on those dictating their confidences to the public letter-writer.

As for the mail itself, in those days it came in all shapes and sizes. Senders, in so far as they considered the matter at all, only had to take account of the most convenient method of folding or wrapping the packet to avoid the possibility of its being mislaid, or the danger of its attracting the attention of potential robbers. The only uniform feature was the use of some sticky substance, usually red wax, to seal the contents and guarantee their privacy.

This sealing wax had another use as well, at a time when illiteracy was the rule rather than the exception. It was customary for people to identify themselves by embossing the wax with a ring or stamp, engraved with the family crest or some such recognisable design. A later innovation was the practice of using red or black oiled ink to mark the place of origin – and sometimes the date as well – on the outside cover. Furthermore, the covers usually had some mark drawing attention to the tax or dues which had to be met on the communication, especially if it had travelled some distance and crossed frontiers.

These letters have become objects of exceptional interest and research for many philatelists, who like using them as a sort of curtain-raiser for their collection of conventional postage stamps. Some of these documents carry instructions to the courier drawing attention to his responsibility for collecting whatever payment is due before handing over the packet. A large zero was the usual mark indicating there was nothing to pay. On the other hand, if the sender had failed to make provision for all the additional dues likely to accumulate on the journey, the accruing charges were added to whatever other instructions were written on the outside, and had to be collected by the courier before the correspondence was handed over. Later, a prepaid or postage-paid (PP) symbol was developed to indicate that revenue charges had been met before the dispatch of the letter (plate 5).

In 1819 the King of Sardinia sponsored a prepaid, inter-territorial postal service. This was really the start of what generally became known as 'paper-post', in contrast to the letter-coupons issued two centuries earlier by the Republic of Venice (plate 1). In 1604 Venice introduced a system for levying charges on correspondence being ferried out of the Republic by canal. These letter-coupons consisted of a printed slip of paper surmounted by the official emblem of Venice, the Lion of St Mark, and the letters AQ (signifying *acque:* water). But the stamped letter-paper issued by the Kingdom of Sardinia approximated more closely the modern concept of a prepaid, franked letter-card (plate 4).

These letter-cards – known to collectors as *Cavallini* (little horses) – were issued in three different denominations, with the nominal value of each clearly

Left: two examples of stamp obliterations bearing both numbers and letters. The letters indicate the post office of origin. Centre: a rare numerical postmark used by Florence around 1785. It is known as 'The Heart of Florence'. Right: a Russian obliteration from Kiev.

indicated. On the outside they bore a blue stamp, which comprised a cherub mounted on a small horse and blowing a post-horn; the figures surrounded by a circular, oval or octagonal rule. The value (15, 25 or 50 centisimi) was clearly marked. Later, the same design was incorporated in an embossed stamp.

The Sardinian letter-paper was not intended to operate as a prepayment on actual delivery: rather, it was a tax charge on the sender. The recipient was still obliged to pay the costs of transporting the letter to him after it had cleared the Sardinian excise control.

It was not until 1840 that steps were taken, in England, to obviate all these impediments to the safe and speedy delivery of the mail; namely, by issuing the first fully stamped prepaid envelopes or covers. These were designed and printed from brass plates engraved by the designer and artist William Mulready, and showed Britannia dispatching messengers (represented as flying angels) to all parts of the world (plate 3).

Despite their potential popularity, few people had the chance of using Mulready covers. Their development coincided with the introduction of a far more convenient and efficient instrument for reforming the postal service: the adhesive-backed postage stamp. The postage stamp, which was specifically designed and introduced to meet general needs, effectively transformed the entire future development of the postal service – and the prospects for philately.

The modern postage stamp

When Rowland Hill, a former school teacher, came up with a proposition for a penny post, it was just what the rising middle class of the nineteenth century wanted. An all-out assault on the corruption and fraud then rife in the public services was urgently needed. 'Pirate' courier services were reckoned to be fleecing the British Treasury of something like one-third of its estimated tax returns.

In 1837 Hill published his proposals for a sweeping reorganisation of the postal service under the title: 'Post Office Reform'. His chief concern was to find a practicable way of reducing the tax burden while at the same time tightening control and improving efficiency. Hill's reforming zeal had been given an extra stimulus by an observation of his friend and colleague, the poet Samuel Taylor Coleridge. Coleridge told Hill that he had witnessed a prime example of another sort of postal fraud altogether. The poet recounted how he had seen 'a poor woman of the people' pleading with a postman for an unstamped letter from her brother. She had been unable to claim the letter as she could not afford to pay the fee. Finally, she persuaded the postman to let her examine the envelope, so as to confirm that it was her brother's handwriting. Then, with tears in her eyes, she returned it to the postman. Coleridge was under the impression that he was watching a distressing example of the crushing effect of poverty on family life.

It was only after Coleridge had offered the woman a shilling to redeem the letter that he discovered what had really happened. The woman explained that the tears were feigned, that in fact she had got all the information she wanted from a quick inspection of the envelope, which was inscribed with a simple code. Inside, the 'letter' consisted of a blank sheet of paper.

Hill saw clearly that this simple, and doubtless widespread, fraud was the logical outcome of an unwieldy postal system. His suggestion was for a flat rate of one penny, regardless of the sort of letter and its destination within the country. Moreover, correspondence was to be stamped *before* dispatch, thereby placing the payment squarely on the sender rather than the recipient. Hence, the postman would be relieved of responsibility for collecting dues.

Hill also insisted on the importance of something more significant, as evidence of payment, than a primitive seal or the cost charge hastily scrawled, in probably illegible handwriting, on some ill-defined part of the outside packet. His first suggestion was for the mandatory provision of prepaid stamped letter-paper, on the lines of the Mulready covers. But he later proposed (some say it

Left: with the early issues of French stamps it is customary to find obliterations in the form of dots, making up rectangles, diamonds or stars. Some of the latter bear figures, which refer to the post office of origin. Right: a French double obliteration.

Some collectors specialise in obliterations made by 'travelling' post offices. Here are two examples: 'Riva Vapore' is the postmark of an Austrian ship from the Kingdom of Lombardy and Venetia, in service on Lake Garda; below, a postmark on letters sent by sea from Venice.

was the idea of a journalist called Chalmers) the manufacture of specially printed coupons of paper, which could be sold to letter-writers in advance, and affixed to the front cover of correspondence by some sort of adhesive gum. This concept led directly – through an Act of Parliament – to the adoption of the gummed postage stamp.

The 'Penny Black', universally recognised as the first postage stamp, was issued 6 May 1840 (plate 6). It bore an engraved portrait of Queen Victoria, and the single word 'POSTAGE' across the top. The value, 'ONE PENNY', was simply marked across the bottom of the stamp between initial letters which differed on each stamp, showing its position in the sheet. On the same date the new postal service issued a second stamp, the 'Twopence Blue'. It bore a similar portrait of Queen Victoria, and was printed in blue, with the necessary change of value. (Both stamps were distributed concurrently with the Mulready stamped letter-paper, which was a prototype of the wrappers customarily used for books, newspapers and samples.)

The design for these, the first stamps, was by the artist Henry Corbould, and was selected from some 2,700 designs submitted from all parts of the country. He received a prize of £500, a considerable sum at the time. The engraving was adopted from the well-known medallion of the Queen by another popular artist of the period, Wyon. The first stamps were imperforate, as the technical means for perforating between each of the stamps in a sheet was not developed for some ten years.

The immediate popularity of the new stamps greatly assisted the wider, general reorganisation of the British postal service, and this lesson was not lost on other states. Switzerland was the first to follow the British example: between 1843 and 1845 series of stamps were issued for the cantons of Zurich, Geneva and Basle. In the same year (1843) Brazil became the first country in the Western Hemisphere to introduce official postage stamps.

Finland entered the lists in 1845, and then in 1847 the first British colonial stamps were issued for the island of Mauritius. Also in 1847, the United States issued stamps of 5- and 10-cent denominations bearing the portraits of Franklin and Washington (plate 24). Following the revolution of 1848 France issued her first stamps (plate 18), and in 1850, while Italy was still subdivided into petty principalities and dukedoms, the first stamps appeared in the Kingdom of Lombardy and Venetia, and in the Grand Duchy of Tuscany (plate 17). At the same time the first German stamps were issued in Prussia, Saxony and Hanover.

Gradually, each nation or state established a particular identity through its postage stamps, either by representing its sovereigns, armorial bearings or characteristic landmarks. These early issues are highly prized by philatelists, not only for their scarcity (and hence monetary value), historical significance and artistic merit, but also for certain qualities of imagination and inspiration which make these stamps unique expressions of national feeling.

Stamps for all purposes

The first stamps were intended as little more than proof that the requisite tax had been paid by those sending letters. It quickly became apparent, however, that the postage stamp had a much greater role to play, and states began introducing wider ranges of stamps, with different categories and values for various purposes.

The first move in this direction was the introduction of a special rate for newspapers and printed matter. Then came special administrative stamps, used exclusively by different departments of state. The degree to which this practice extended varied from country to country, but it embraced customs and excise, the police, civil service, local government and the armed forces. In time of emergency and war, the armed forces of different countries have frequently improvised and imposed their own methods for maintaining the priority of military communications, often by means of simple rubber franks to approve the passage of military correspondence

An oval, numerical obliteration with a Jersey date stamp. English post offices used these obliterations between 1860 and 1885 (approx.).

Two nineteenth-century obliterations, characteristically British. The first is a Maltese Cross, which was stamped, either in red or in black, on the earliest issues; the second, one of the many numeral obliterations used by the British post office in Montevideo, Uruguay (1862–72).

without the use of formal postal issues. At other times, during political upheavals or revolutions, a new administration has frequently overprinted the existing range of postage stamps with a rubber stamp, indicating the changed situation (plates 76, 80, 87, 91, 100).

The application of stamps has been further increased by scientific advances, and particularly by the development of new forms of communication (telegraph and telephone). Special supplementary stamps have also been issued for a variety of purposes, from the prevention of tax-dodging to the promotion of commercial organisations, and even as a form of credit. The range of special stamps has varied from country to country. In Britain, for example, there have been special post office stamps for savings, as well as for the national insurance and health services. Other countries have issued stamps to indicate the granting of special concessions and privileges, or in the case of the United States the *abolition* of the franking privilege held by government departments until 1873. This change resulted in the use of official stamps inscribed with the individual department names.

Far more important than the stamps issued for the holders of special concessions and private enterprises was the introduction of the first special airmail stamps. Italy was the first country to issue an airmail stamp, in honour of the first officially recognised delivery of mail by air, in May 1917. The United States followed a year later, with the first regular issue of airmail stamps.

Collectors have also shown particular interest in those stamps used in exceptional circumstances, such as the use of aircraft to break a military blockade or leap-frog enemy forces. Four years before the French revolution, an attempt was made on 7 January 1785, by the famous balloonist Blanchard, to carry mail from Britain to France. Almost ten years later, a balloon was also used to send messages of support and encouragement to the people of Lombardy, who were fighting to free themselves from Austrian domination. In 1870, what was virtually a regular balloon postal service was set up when Paris was surrounded and besieged by Prussian armies. Later, balloons and dirigibles, particularly Germany's famous Zeppelins, played a crucial part in the development of airmail transport before the effective development of passenger- and mail-carrying aircraft.

The impact made by aviation has been reflected in the widespread practice of issuing special airmail stamps, most notably in commemoration of solo and long distance flights (plate 31). Among these are tributes to the Wright brothers, the first crossing of the English Channel by Louis Bleriot, the first Atlantic crossing from east to west by the British aviators Alcock and Brown, and the first solo flight from the United States to France by Colonel Charles Lindbergh in the *Spirit of St Louis*.

Commemorative stamps

Before very many years passed, stamps began to acquire a more general significance than was at first apparent. The exclusive reproduction of national emblems or the likeness of contemporary monarchs gave way to designs of wider educational, if not actual propaganda, significance. Stamps were an excellent means for promoting national pride and civic dignity. They were also a convenient way of paying homage to the past, recalling highlights of national history and international affairs, and acknowledging the contributions and achievements of the great, from sovereigns to savants. All that was required was to issue a special range or series of stamps.

Peru was probably the first country to issue a commemorative stamp. In April 1871 a special Peru 5 centavo, red was printed in honour of the first Latin-American railway linking Lima and Callao. It represented a railway engine, and was captioned 'Chorillos-Lima-Callao', even though the Callao terminus was not actually reached until 1879.

In 1876 the United States struck a special issue to commemorate the centenary of the Declaration of Independence, and then in 1893 issued a special set of 16

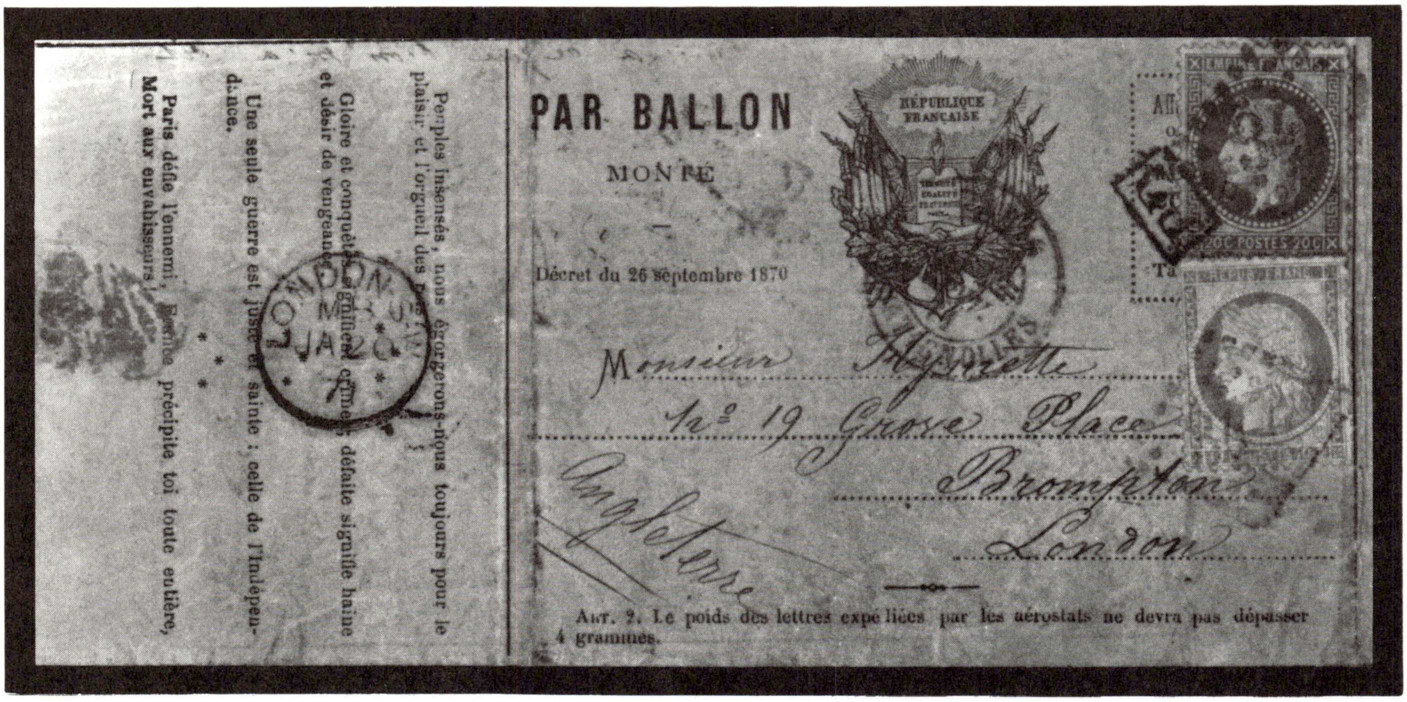
PAR BALLON
MONTE
RÉPUBLIQUE FRANÇAISE
Décret du 26 septembre 1870
Monsieur
No 19 Grove Place
Brompton
London
Angleterre
ART. 2. Le poids des lettres expédiées par les aérostats ne devra pas dépasser 4 grammes.

EXPRESS WELLS FARGO
Precio,
FRANCO EN LA
REPUBLICA MEXICANA
Y POR TODAS LAS LINEAS DE LA COMPAÑIA
NEW YORK
JUN 5
7 30 PM
89
via New York
Julius Cyriax Esq
16. Coleman Street
E.C. London
Inglaterra

The means by which an envelope was transported can greatly increase its interest (and value). Left are two fascinating examples. Top: a London-bound letter carried out of Paris by balloon, during the siege of 1870–1; note the defiant slogans on the cover. Below: an envelope carried by Wells Fargo from Mexico to New York, where it received a US postage stamp and continued its journey to England (1889).

different values to mark the 400th anniversary of the discovery of America. In 1888 New South Wales followed the American lead by issuing stamps on the 100th anniversary of the founding of the colony. It is interesting to note that Great Britain – in contrast to some of her colonies – continued to issue stamps bearing the royal effigy, and *only* such stamps, until well into the middle of the twentieth century. France issued her first commemoratives in 1923: a series of three different values marking the centenary of the birth of the famous scientist, Louis Pasteur (plate 102). Shortly afterwards, a stamp in the current series of conventional issues was overprinted to commemorate the Philatelic Congress then being held in Bordeaux.

From that time onwards, commemorative stamps have flowed off the presses in an ever-increasing stream. Virtually every event of national or world importance (and many of scant significance) has been represented by the issue of special stamps. The reasons, as already indicated, are not difficult to find. To begin with, there is considerable educational value in portraying historical incidents and individuals of special significance. Moreover, it is a matter of national pride to do so. Finally, and not least important, postal authorities make considerable profit from the sale of special issues. Indeed, such issues constitute almost a forced tax so far as philatelists are concerned, although their appeal is much wider than that. They can be items of rare beauty. Modern methods of printing, particularly colour printing, make it possible to reproduce works of art, costumes, landscapes and so on to a quite extraordinarily high standard.

However, collectors still tend to regard the first quarter of the twentieth century as the golden age of commemorative stamps. The issues of this period were designed and engraved by some of the greatest artists of the time, and collectors specialising in stamps of this period are still inclined to acknowledge the technical achievements of modern photogravure with a tinge of regret.

How stamps are printed

Postage stamps reproduce either drawings or photographs, although the method of printing, the means by which hundreds of thousands, or even tens of millions of an issue are manufactured, varies considerably. It should be pointed out, however, that while it is usual to think of stamps rolling off government or private printing presses in such enormous quantities, this is not always the case. There have been times when only a limited number of a certain issue has been required. This was particularly true in the early days of postage stamps, and it is the scarcity of such issues (in some cases only *one* example remains in existence) that gives them such a high commercial value.

It must also be remembered that stamps have sometimes had to be improvised by the crudest means to meet exceptional situations. Isolated outposts, temporarily cut off from their main communications centres, have been forced to issue substitute stamps; likewise, irregular issues have appeared in circumstances of national emergency, by provisional administrations, occupying forces and revolutionaries seizing power. In such extraordinary circumstances any available means to hand have been pressed into service: rubber or metal stamping has been the most common improvisation, using small rectangles of white or tinted paper or even ordinary labels. Sometimes the values have been handwritten in ink and initialled by the post office clerk. Type-written emergency issues are also known.

However, postage stamps, in the classic sense, have usually been printed by the most sophisticated methods: letterpress, lithography and, most recently, photogravure and offset lithography. Naturally, the production of postage stamps requires much detailed preparatory work. There are the preliminary 'roughs', sketches, photographs and proofs to be examined and approved; the most suitable printing technique, paper, watermark and perforation all must be decided upon.

When lithographic reproduction is required the final

An envelope carried by Zeppelin airship on the occasion of the Danzig International Airmail Exhibition, 1932.

approved design is reproduced on a large lithographic stone and, using a special transfer method, repeated in many rows of perfectly aligned images to form the printing surface. Once this has been done, a whole sheet of identical stamps can be printed simultaneously. When letterpress printing was used initially, the design had to be meticulously engraved in metal for every single stamp from a highly finished hand-drawn original. In letterpress printing today the photo engraving method makes possible all kinds of combinations of image and letters or figures. The same image may be used for the whole series with simple changes of the values.

A third process is known as photogravure. A number of small photographic reproductions of the original designs, sufficient to form a sheet (usually 400), is reproduced on a special paper and then transferred on to a copper cylinder, on a part of the rotary gravure printing press. Offset lithography is based on substituting for the lithographic stone a metal plate, which is wrapped around a cylinder in the printing machine.

Every method can be expected to produce occasional and unforeseen errors: a matrix may chip or break, type become displaced, and spelling or grammatical errors escape the notice of proof-readers (plates 53, 56, 57, 58, 61). There may also be occasional variations of colour, or the printing machine may stop momentarily, leaving a blot, or slightly heavier or lighter impression. Usually these faults are eliminated as soon as possible and the stamps destroyed, but sometimes they escape notice until the stamps are on sale. Defacements and errors give some postage stamps special rarity and value, and in certain cases defacements have been deliberately contrived or procured with the intention of exploiting the financial advantages likely to accrue from their rarity value.

Another aspect of postage stamp production to which collectors pay close attention is the form and measurement of the perforation marks along the sides of stamps. Variations or changes in the scale of the gauge may significantly affect the market value of a stamp. Many early stamps had no perforation, but there have been occasions when normally perforated stamps have been printed and distributed to post offices without perforation, as a result of a fault in the perforating machine. Naturally, stamp speculators are quick to cash in on such errors, as well as on mistakes in design, misprints or inking variations.

Organising a collection

There can be few people who have not, at one time or another, been attracted by the beauty of postage stamps. But the almost universal interest in stamps is stimulated not only by outstanding colour and design; it stems in large measure from the extraordinary variety of subjects represented by them. Virtually everything has been dealt with: dogs, cats, flowers, butterflies, minerals, landscapes, doctors, artists, writers, musicians and musical instruments, transport and machines, heroes and saints, captains and kings, tyrants and despots, clothes and furniture, sculpture and design, vintage car and railway engines, weapons, fruit, fish, even snatches of music and prose. The list could be extended almost indefinitely. Stamps are associated with every kind of adventure and excitement; they are the links of history; they give validity and reality to rare moments of historical and political drama in the life of one's own nation and of far-distant peoples. This is the spirit that informs and fosters the passion for philately.

As a rule, the novice collector starts off by putting his stamps into boxes or envelopes. But as the number and variety of specimens increases there is inevitably an urge to sort them into categories, and display them properly arranged and marked up, even if, in the first instance, only a common exercise book is available. Naturally, interest increases with the number of stamps accumulated, and the extent to which the names and varieties from little known places and people are added to the more familiar. The time soon comes when it is essential to give the collection greater style and shape, as well as a more definitive character. At this point a choice

has to be made between the different methods and equipment available. The collector must decide whether to settle for some sort of conventional stick-in album, or adopt a newer method, such as the stock-book system. So many different types of albums and classification systems are now available to tempt the beginner that the choice is not always easy. Unhappily, there is no obvious 'best' system.

In the first place there are the conventional fixed-leaf albums, usually illustrated with a number of stamp issues in black and white. But these obviously cannot accommodate all the different series of stamps issued, although an interesting collection may be made simply by sticking to the limited objective of obtaining really good specimens of the series illustrated. Then there are the larger, loose-leaf albums, which can be expanded to take a far wider range of varieties. Moreover, there are any number of specialist albums which make provision for certain series or individual stamps.

All these albums have one factor in common. The collector is obliged to fix the stamps in position by means of small slips of gummed paper known as stamp hinges, or transparent envelopes with an opaque black or white backing (plate 167). The stock-book method is in marked contrast. To begin with, stamps which may occupy anything from two to six pages in conventional albums may be displayed on a single sheet in the stock-book type of presentation (plate 165). It must be pointed out, however, that the principal characteristic of this method (specimens are held in position by means of long transparent strips) puts a premium on overcrowding and overlapping, and therefore increases the risk of damage. Furthermore, it is not possible, without leaving an untidy impression, to leave space for missing specimens in any given series, as it is in those albums that are ruled up in squares (sometimes even with special positions for 'sets') and require hinges. On the other hand, the outstanding advantage of this method is that the need for hinges is obviated. Hence, there is far less risk of superficial damage to the gum.

Whatever method of display is chosen, it is vital for all collectors to know the best way of treating stamps to avoid defacing or injuring them. Unused stamps clearly require the most careful handling, if only because any damage is so immediately obvious. But it is equally important because of the need to protect the condition of the original gum. The main reason why philatelists pay so much attention to the gum is that it is susceptible to mildew, which poses a serious threat to the general condition of the collection if it is allowed to take root.

This is why collectors are always strongly recommended to use only stamp hinges if they are fastening their specimens into fixed positions. The tiny slips of paper not only allow the stamps to be fixed neatly into place, but leave the backs open for easy inspection, and allow the air to circulate, thereby minimising the dangers of damp and rot.

There are some who decry the use of hinges, insisting that any trace of additional material on the back of a stamp seriously detracts from its appearance and worth. On the other hand, the current trend among some of the most advanced collectors, particularly in the United States, is to wash the gum off *all* stamps, used and unused alike. This certainly does decrease the possibility of serious deterioration, but it must be pointed out that the market value of such a stamp can suffer as a result.

There can be no doubt that the care and attention given to the conditions under which any collection is maintained play a fundamental part in its preservation and appearance. It is essential to make sure that stamps are kept in well aired and ventilated rooms. Albums should never be locked away in damp attics or humid cupboards; nor should they be left for any length of time in sealed envelopes or plastic or cellophane containers. It is important to cultivate the habit of treating collections with care, never handling stamps with damp or wet fingers, or moistening the fingertips to turn the pages of an album, or picking up hinges without using tweezers.

If by any chance there is reason to fear that a collection has become infected by rot, it is sometimes a useful palliative to soak the threatened stamps in purified spirit, such as is used to examine water-marks. The white spirit will kill fungi and most types of rot, without damaging the surface or ink, even of unused specimens.

Used stamps are much easier to look after because of the absence of gum. However, great care must be exercised in detaching them from the envelopes or postcards to which they may be fixed. There is also an inevitable danger, as with washing clothes, of the colours running. The collector comes to know by experience the best way of unsticking specimens. Warm water is the most efficient, but care must be taken, with certain stamps, not to damage their colour. Also, special attention must be paid to the unsticking process when dealing with stamps glued on to glazed paper, especially if it has been coated with some species of kaolin. It is always a good idea to float the morsels of paper on to the surface of the water in a shallow dish. If the stamp is face upwards, it is possible to avoid wetting the upper surface.

Once stamps have been separated from the paper, they should be put to dry on blotting paper, again face upwards. It is also important to avoid the temptation to accelerate the drying process by putting the wet stamps on radiators or in the sun. If too much heat is applied, stamps curl up at the edges and become more friable. The sun is particularly dangerous, as the rays affect colour in a very short time and the dye fades.

The other major problems facing the collector are how to avoid the oxidation of ink, and the stains which produce the effect of 'yellowing' or 'rusting'; in other

Mail carried by Francis Chichester from Lord Howe Island to Neutral Bay (Sydney) during his flight across the Tasman Sea, 1931.

words, how to avoid the ravages of time. Pink, yellow and orange inks are those most likely to be affected by oxydisation, and this phenomenon is well known to specialists who collect the stamps issued by the Kingdom of Naples in 1858. These stamps, of a rose-carmine tint, are particularly sensitive, and are known to develop a brownish variation in colour. As for yellowing, or the rust spots that may appear, these are simply part of the ageing process that affects old books, and indeed all paper products. The best way of retarding any of these developments is to ensure, as already mentioned, that stamps be maintained under well ventilated conditions.

Some collectors not only specialise in certain stamps but gather together, on the pages of their albums, all sorts of related material. In addition to similar stamps from other countries there could even be different qualities of paper, different colours and inks, gums and watermarks.

Some enthusiasts concentrate on collecting only one particular type of stamp, portrait, effigy or design. This involves considerable time and research to obtain the maximum number of individual specimens, either in unused or used condition. They may be unattached or still fastened to their envelopes or wrappers. A collection of this sort may run into thousands if the study is extended to obtaining examples of the same stamp posted from different towns, villages, and countries, each listed separately with details of the respective post offices from which they were dispatched, and displayed in alphabetical order, together with franking marks, obliterations, cancellations, defacements, watermarks, superscriptions, surcharges and so forth.

In such circumstances it is easy to understand why the 1851 issue of the United States, or the fourth series of Sardinian stamps, may each require one, or even more, albums. Anyone who decides to concentrate on collecting the well-known French issue of Napoleon III, complete with all the obliterations of the star-shaped dotted postmarks, may need as many as a dozen albums.

Any collector committed to this type of specialisation will find himself involved in a great deal of study and research, not to mention the time spent on cleaning, classifying and mounting the stamps, letters and other fragments associated with the study. These specialists obviously require either loose-leaf albums or capacious filing systems; and, even then, they frequently come across problems of treatment and display which can only be solved through experience.

Used and unused; forgeries and fakes

The relative value of used and unused stamps is a major issue in philately, and one that all new enthusiasts would like to have resolved with a simple guide-rule. Unfortunately, one does not exist. Some unused stamps are worth ten times a used example, while other used specimens are far more valuable than equivalent unused ones. A convenient example is a Postmasters' stamp issued for Rhode Island in 1846 (a year before the first US issue). The 5c black is valued at £28 ($70) unused, but when obliterated is worth as much as £180 ($450). In contrast, the US 5c red-orange of 1847 (a rare shade) is worth £1,100 ($2,750) unused but only £150 ($375) used. It all depends on the number of stamps printed at any time, and how long they remain in circulation. The more that are issued, and the longer they stay in use, the greater the premium placed on unused examples.

There is no doubt, however, that for many collectors unused stamps hold a special attraction. They look neat and clean, whereas used specimens are frequently dirty, defaced, and often virtually unrecognisable as a result of the obliterations. But a used stamp has, after all, fulfilled the function for which it was printed. Furthermore, the collection of used stamps is not only easier (in most respects), but it is probably less costly than always insisting on unused ones.

Postage stamps are by no means immune from fraud and fakery, and there are forged stamps in circulation just as there are forged bank notes. A clear distinction is made, however, between different types of false stamps. There are forgeries designed to defraud the postal service (plate 92), and there are forgeries designed to deceive collectors. The 'genuine' postal forgeries are, generally speaking, much sought by philatelists. They can acquire quite astonishing value, especially if they can be proved (by their obliteration marks) to have actually been used for postage. In contrast, the philatelic forgery poses a serious threat to collectors. Anyone suspicious about the origins of a stamp in his possession would do well to consult an expert.

There also exists a whole range of deceptive practices, such as false superscriptions, obliteration marks and perforations. A typical example of this was the practice of reversing the effigies in some issues of stamps put out by Sardinia and by the provisional government of Naples in the last century. Of course when such errors are authentic mistakes they are rare and valuable, whereas stamps deliberately manufactured with anomalies have very little value.

There is also the question of repairing stamps. It is sometimes, though rarely, possible to patch up a slightly damaged stamp by adding a few marks or perforation points. It is also possible to clean or renovate other aspects by, say, touching up the surface, or filling in some minute particle which may have been torn or scraped off. Such a patched-up stamp may not be worthless, although it will certainly not have more than a fraction of its catalogue value. Repaired or second quality stamps are chiefly of interest to collectors who want them for their own satisfaction rather than their commercial value. The collector who is not in a position to afford first quality specimens of, for example, the famous French 1849 one franc vermillion, or the 1847 10c black, first issue of the United States, may be quite contented with an imperfect example available at a greatly reduced price.

Bibliography

Periodicals:

Stamp Monthly, Stanley Gibbons Magazines Ltd, Drury House, Russell Street, London WC2B 5HD, England.
Stamp Magazine, Link House Publications Ltd, Dingwall Avenue, Croydon CR9 2TA, Surrey, England.
Stamp Collecting, Harris Publications, 42 Maiden Lane, London WC2, England.
Philatelic Magazine, Harris Publications, 42 Maiden Lane, London WC2, England.
American Philatelist, 5932 North 14th Place, Phoenix, Arizona 85014, USA.
Stamps, H. L. Lindquist Publications Inc, 153 Waverley Place, New York 10014, USA.
Linns Weekly Stamp News, Sydney Ptg and Publ Co, PO Box 29, Sydney, Ohio 45365, USA.
National Stamp News, PO Box 696, Anderson, South Carolina 29621, USA.

Catalogues:

Scott: Volumes I, II and III, Worldwide. New York 1972.
Stanley Gibbons: British Commonwealth. London 1972. Stamps of the World. London 1972. United States and Possessions. London 1971.

1

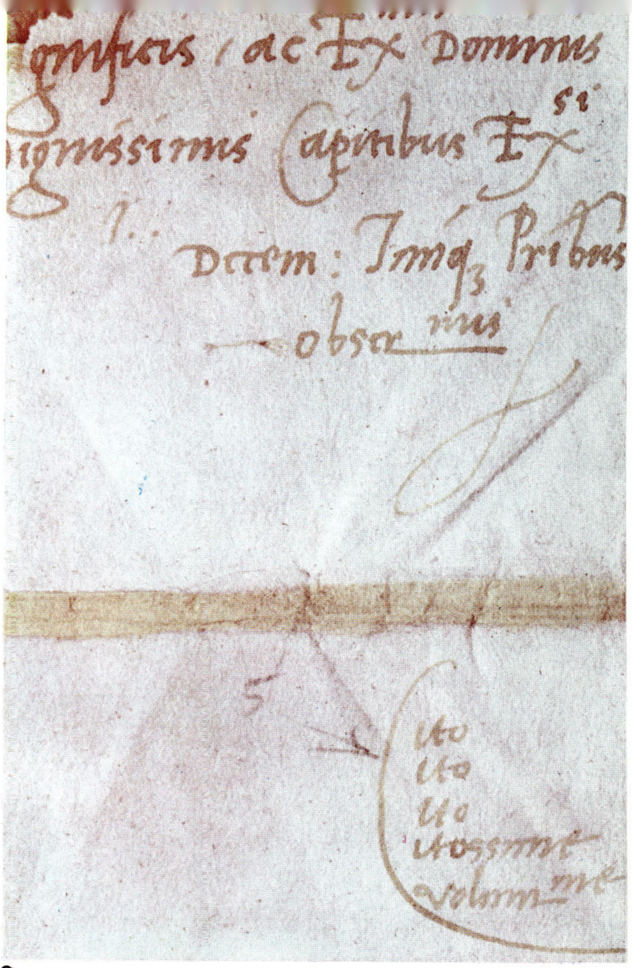

2

3

4

5

1 Three examples of the first taxed letter-coupons, which were introduced by the Republic of Venice at the beginning of the seventeenth century. They are known to collectors as 'AQ forms'.

2 Between the years 1200 and 1400 letters were transported by mounted couriers, who were under constant pressure to speed-up delivery. This fragment of a letter bears the usual exhortation: *'cito, cito, cito, citissime, volantissime'* ('Quick, quick, quick! Hurry up! Fly!)

3 A 'Mulready'. These covers, issued at one penny or twopence, were put into service in Britain at the same time as Rowland Hill's postage stamps were introduced.

4 A Sardinian *Cavallini*. These water-marked postcards were provisionally issued in 1819. The definitive issue, in 1820, differed from the original in that it was impressed in relief, by an embossing stamper.

5 A good French example of early prepaid postal franking, before the issue of adhesive postage stamps.

6

6 The 'Penny Black', issued by Great Britain in 1840: the first adhesive postage stamp in the world.

7 A typical letter before the introduction of adhesive postage stamps. The issuing authority, the police of the Grand Duchy of Tuscany, and the town of origin, Florence, are both stamped on the cover.

8 Before the introduction of state postal services, courier delivery was in the hands of private companies and agencies. This letter carries the seal of a well-known diligence delivery service, L. Orcesi. It is addressed to the director in charge of pontifical diligences at Bologna.

9 Philatelists take a particular interest in pre-postage stamp examples of state communications, especially if they contain military or political information. This Venetian letter, dated 5 July 1849 and marked '*Urgentissima*', confirms the existence of the new and short-lived Republic of Venice.

10 A rare proof of an early stamp, designed by Riester for the first Bolivian series (1864). The design was not adopted, but it is a typical example of the preparatory work that goes into the production of postage stamps: the selection of designs submitted by competing artists and engravers, the supervision and approval of print and ink, the choice of paper, water-marks and perforations.

10

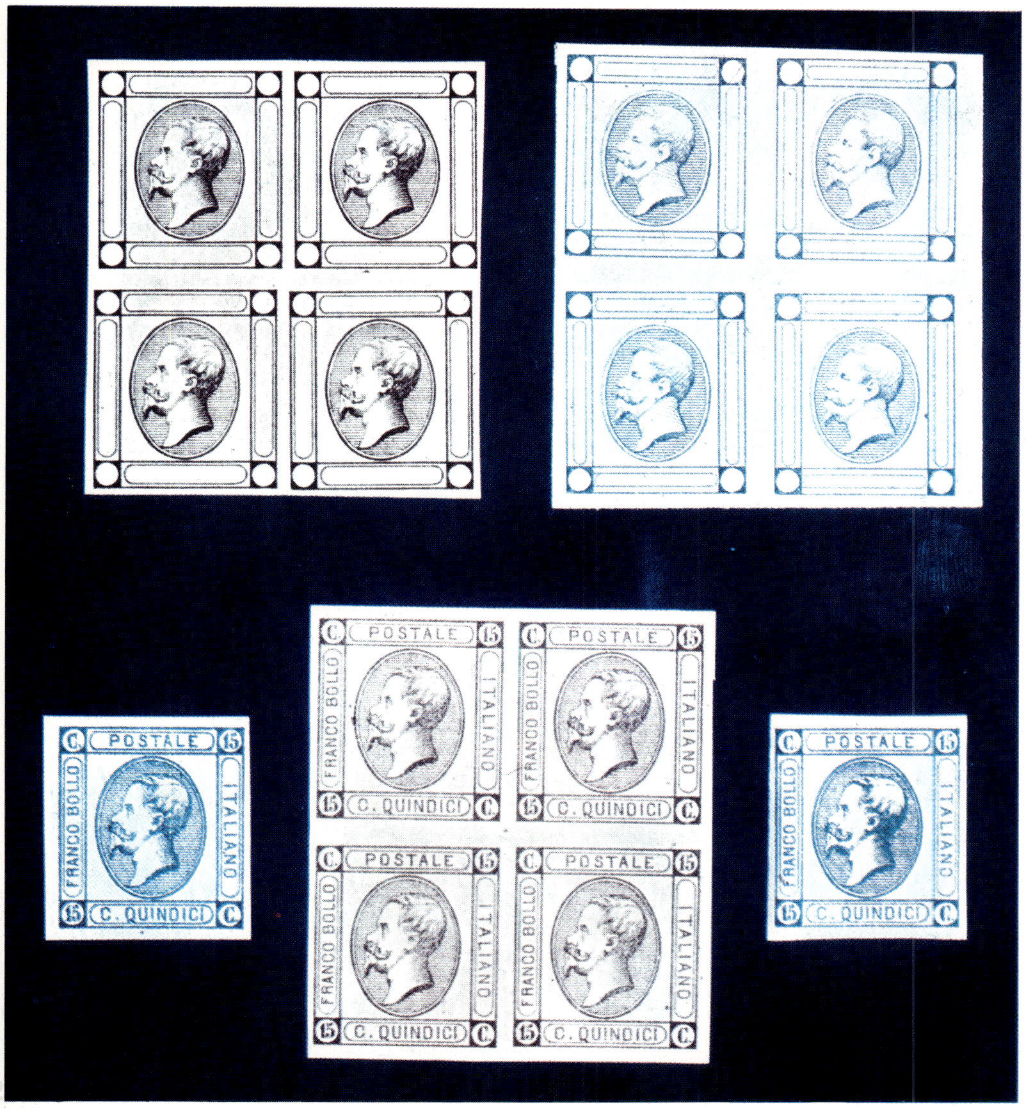

11 A good example of the stages in the printing of a postage stamp, in this case the '15 centisimi lithograph' (1863). This is the first true Italian postage stamp, the first to use the words 'POSTALE ITALIANO', and was printed by the typographer Matraire of Turin. The illustration shows the first proof in black, without inscriptions, and then the blue proof, also without inscriptions; beneath them is the final black proof, flanked by two examples of the finished stamp.

12 A block of eight samples of a proof for the French 25 centimes, yellow-brown. It was not accepted.

13 An Italian royal decree authorising the preparation of a new stamp, the 20 centesimi, blue.

14 An essay (suggested design) for an early Italian stamp, printed in the royal colours, with embossed lettering standing out in white relief.

15 A proof of a rare coloured impression of the 5 centesimi stamp of the famous Italian 1863 series, put out by the British printers and postage-stamp specialists, De La Rue.

16 Four coloured proofs of the Italian 20 centesimi, 1866, printed by De La Rue.

17 In a classic stamp collection, the pages of greatest interest tend to be those showing the earliest issues. The first Italian stamps were issued in 1850, when Italy was still divided into petty kingdoms and dukedoms. Included here are stamps from the Kingdom of Naples, bearing the Trinacrie, and a Sicilian stamp bearing the portrait of the Bourbon ruler, King Ferdinand; early issues for Lombardy and Venetia, with the Austrian eagle, and a selection of stamps from Modena and Parma, from the provisional government of Romagna, the Kingdom of Sardinia, the Grand Duchy of Tuscany as well as the provisional government of the unified Italian state.

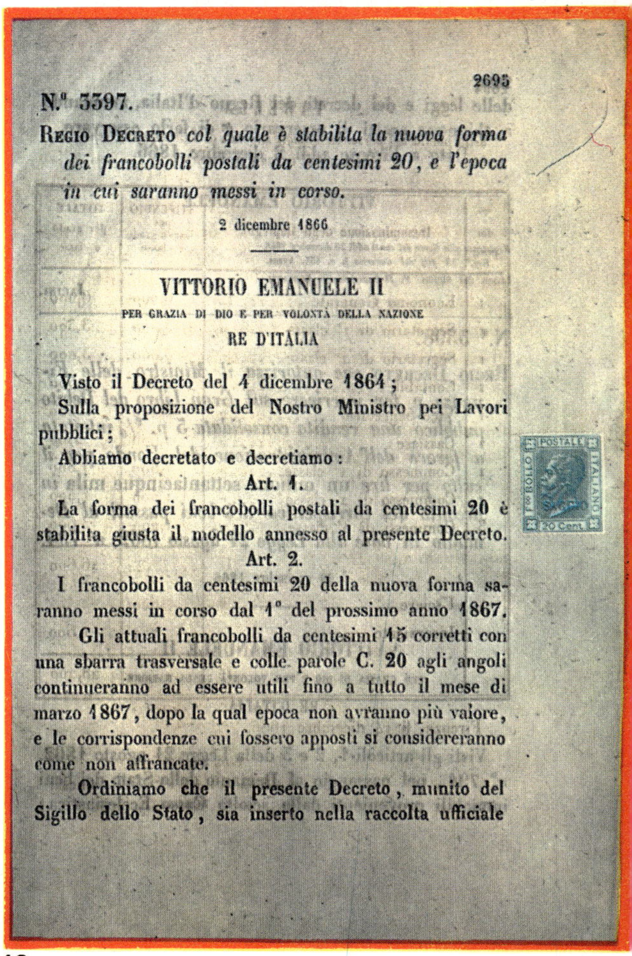

N.° 3397. 2695

REGIO DECRETO *col quale è stabilita la nuova forma dei francobolli postali da centesimi 20, e l'epoca in cui saranno messi in corso.*

2 dicembre 1866

VITTORIO EMANUELE II

PER GRAZIA DI DIO E PER VOLONTÀ DELLA NAZIONE

RE D'ITALIA

Visto il Decreto del 4 dicembre 1864;

Sulla proposizione del Nostro Ministro pei Lavori pubblici;

Abbiamo decretato e decretiamo:

Art. 1.

La forma dei francobolli postali da centesimi 20 è stabilita giusta il modello annesso al presente Decreto.

Art. 2.

I francobolli da centesimi 20 della nuova forma saranno messi in corso dal 1° del prossimo anno 1867.

Gli attuali francobolli da centesimi 15 corretti con una sbarra trasversale e colle parole C. 20 agli angoli continueranno ad essere utili fino a tutto il mese di marzo 1867, dopo la qual epoca non avranno più valore, e le corrispondenze cui fossero apposti si considereranno come non affrancate.

Ordiniamo che il presente Decreto, munito del Sigillo dello Stato, sia inserto nella raccolta ufficiale

13

14 15

18 Four examples of the first French issue (1849–50), representing Ceres crowned with a laurel wreath. They were engraved by Jean-Jacques Barre, and printed by hand.

19 Examples of the rare 80 centimes *tête-bêche* (head to tail), a French stamp (issued 1853–60) in which Napoleon III's effigy has replaced Ceres. These stamps are known as the 'presidency series'.

16

POSTA
GRA 1
POSTA
GR 2
POSTA
G 2
POSTE ESTENSI
CENT. 5.
15 CENTES.
STATI PARM
FRANCO BOLLO POSTALE
½
BAI.
ROMAGNE
C. POSTE. 20.
FRANCO
BOLLO
C. VENTI
C POSTE 40
FRANCO
BOLLO
QUARANTA
POSTALE
FRANCOBOLLO
TOSCANO
20 CENT
10. Cent.

7

REPUB. FRANC.
Banquiers

Lima.

18 19

20

21

20 New postage stamps were issued to mark the accession of King Victor Emmanuel II to the throne of a unified Italy (1861). The top five were never issued, but those below went into regular service in the province of Naples.

21 An interesting selection of early French stamps, all bearing the head of Napoleon III. At the top left is an example dating from the Second Republic (Louis Napoleon was president) while the others all date from the Second Empire; in the later issues the Emperor is crowned with laurels. The adoption of perforations is noteworthy, as is the marginal corner pair and the block of four with sheet margin attached.

22 This block of six is from an incomplete series, issued by the Vatican during the occupation of Rome (1870); these examples, however, are considered to be printer's rejects.

23 Stamps issued by the Kingdom of Naples were suppressed after its downfall in 1860. But impressions such as these, particularly when grouped in different values, are highly prized by collectors.

24 The 5 cent Franklin and 10 cent Washington were the first regular United States issues, replacing the earlier Postmaster's Provisionals. Issued in 1847, they remained in circulation for four years. The two stamps at the bottom right are special official imitations printed in 1875 for the Centennial Exposition the following year. They were not valid for postal purposes.

22 23

24

25

25 As is the case with Italy, stamps from the old German states, prior to the unification of Germany, are extremely rare and valuable. Several of the states printed in black on coloured paper: two specimens from Oldenburg; below them, three from Saxony; further down, three from Württemberg. The use of different colours for stamps of different value within the same series was quite ingenious, and indeed, all these stamps are fine examples of craftsmanship.

26

26 In postal history, 'Thurn und Taxis' stamps are of special interest. They were issued by the Tasso family, which had held a monopoly on mail services over much of Europe for several centuries. This private postal service was still in existence in a few German states during the early days of postage stamps. These stamps are very distinctive, with the value of each clearly marked in the centre; the earliest issues were printed in black on coloured paper, whereas the later issues were printed in colour on white paper.

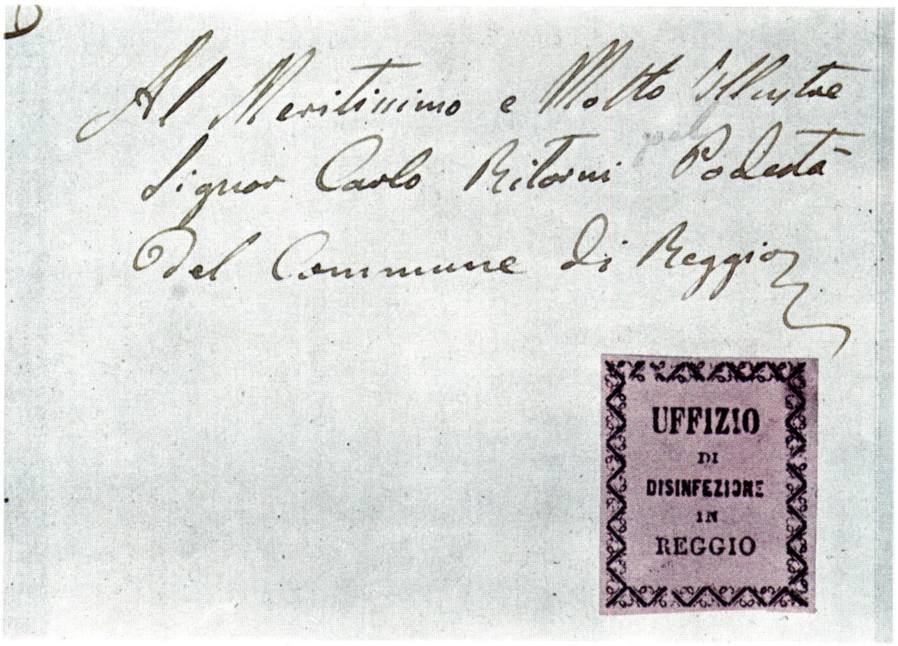

27

28

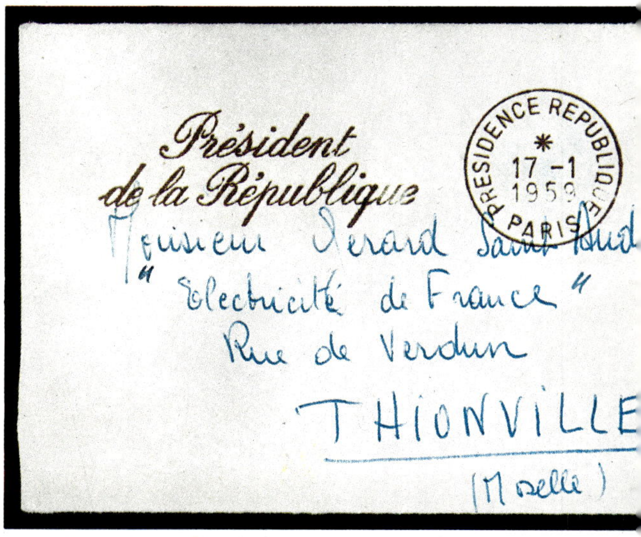

29

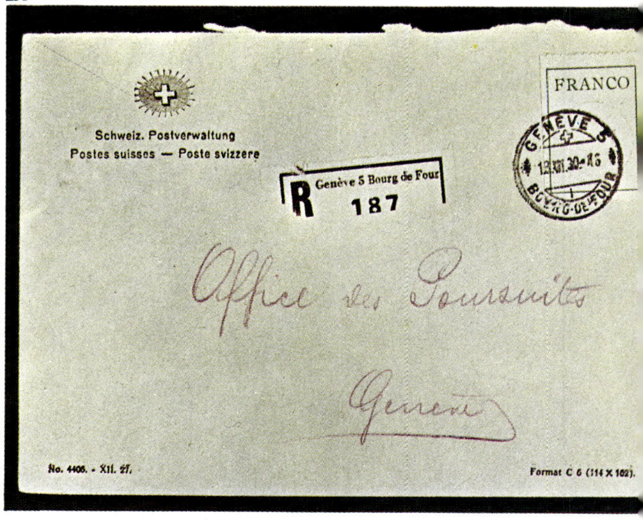

30

31

27 Letters had to be decontaminated during epidemics, particularly epidemics of cholera and plague. Here is an example of an early adhesive administrative stamp (not to be confused with a postage stamp) of the health decontamination bureau at Reggio Emilia, Italy.

28 Traditionally, governmental departments and high officials of state have not been required to use postage stamps. Here is an example of a letter from the President of the French Republic, franked at the Elysées Palace, Paris.

29 An example of registered post from Switzerland. Instead of bearing an actual postage stamp it has been printed with a special indication, 'FRANCO', to show that it has been officially franked and issued under the state prerogative.

30 Decontamination offices were still functioning after the introduction of postage stamps. This letter carries a franking mark indicating it is 'clean, inside and out'.

31 Rare Italian airmail stamps issued to commemorate early transatlantic crossings.

32 A page of unused German airmail stamps issued between 1919 and 1923. These simple stamps, monotypes for the most part, are not of great commercial value, but they do represent for many the 'golden age' of philately, a time when stamps were not judged by their market price.

ALLEMAGNE

TIMBRES POUR LA POSTE AÉRIENNE

1919. — Cor de poste ou biplan. Dentelés 14.

1922-23. — Aigle. Fil. lignes ondulées entrecroisées. Dentelés 14.

Dentelés 13 × 13½.

Unicolores.

33

33 Three examples of special 'express' delivery Italians, the first (top left) issued in 1903 to supersede the old custom of handwritten exhortations urging the need for speed, or claiming special priority from the courier.

34 An example of the special letter-cards issued for the French pneumatic personal delivery service. *Pneutmatiques*, in some respects the precursors of telegrams, were a nineteenth-century French innovation by which mail could be dispatched through an underground complex of special-bore tubes, linking one post office to another. The correspondence was placed in small tubular containers, exactly fitting the pipes, and propelled by an advanced system of compressed air. It was then delivered by express messenger from the point nearest the designated address.

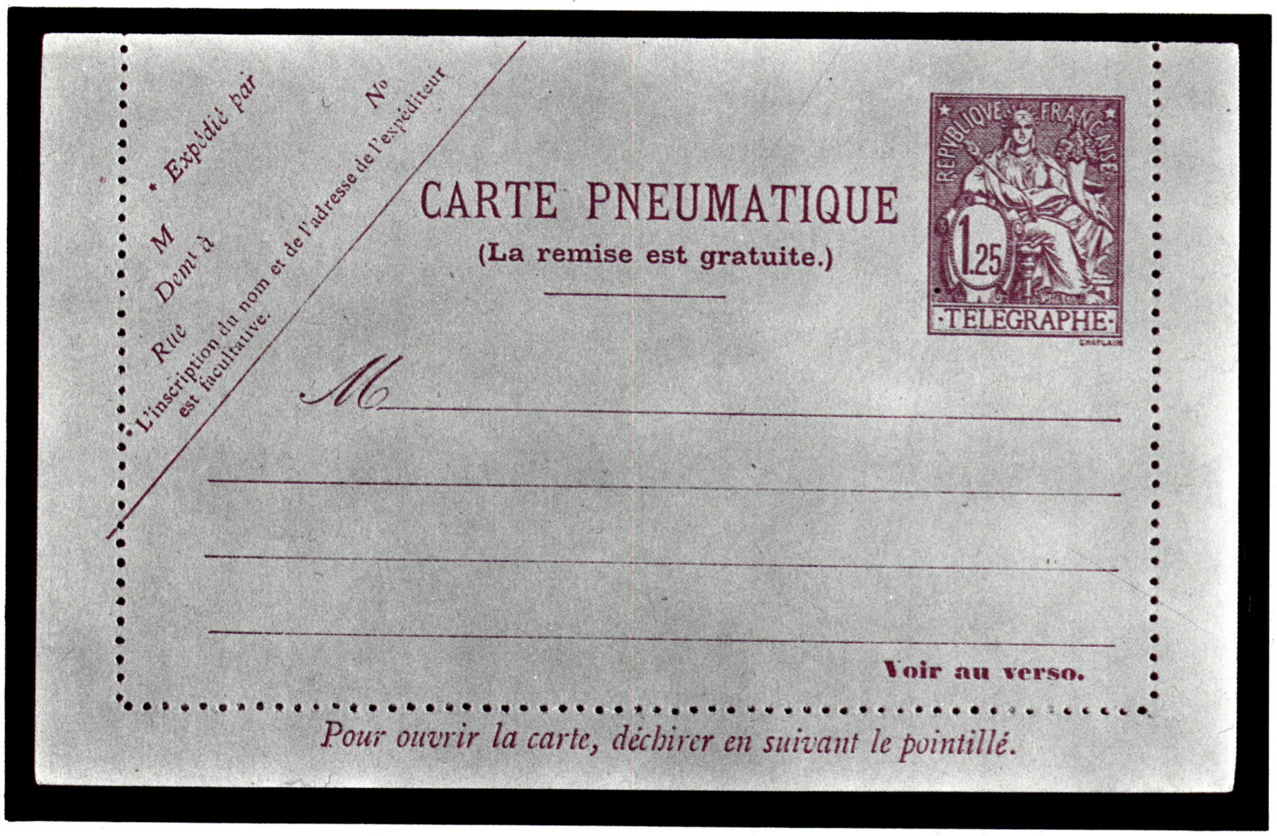

34

35

35 Not all countries felt the need to produce special stamps for newspaper or printed paper rates. The examples shown here consist of Austrian paper stamps, of comparatively low value, bearing the head of the god Mercury. The triangular stamp in the middle was issued in 1916 as a special 'newspaper express' stamp. After the collapse of the Austro-Hungarian Empire, at the end of the First World War, these and many other stamps of the same period were overprinted 'DEUTSCHÖSTERREICH' (Austro-Germany).

36
37

36 Airmail stamps are much sought, and indeed there are collectors who specialise in them. Some of these Italian issues are not only airmail stamps but commemoratives as well.

37 A series of three Italian stamps issued for an experimental pneumatic service (see plate 34).

38

38 A selection of Israeli airmail issues. Collectors pay a premium for those attached to a complementary tab, a particularly attractive feature of some Israeli stamps.

39

39 Special parcel post stamps were not issued until some years after the introduction of postage stamps. They generally took the form of a single stamp, but some countries adopted a system of double stamping. One portion of these Italian 'doubles' accompanies the parcel; the other is retained by the sender as proof of payment.

41

40 This Belgian parcel post stamp issued in 1902 is distinguished by a 'winged wheel' from a railway engine, to indicate the link between parcel post and railway freightage.

41 Advertising stamps, introduced in Italy between 1910 and 1924, were sandwiched between ordinary postage stamps.

42 Pre-stamped French publicity postcards were sold for considerably less than the value of the stamp itself.

43

43 Postcards issued during the First World War for use by French (or Franco-Russian) armies. Note that the middle one has been defaced: the Imperial Russian eagle has been deleted by the Kerensky government following the February Revolution (1917).

44

45

46

44-45 Examples of the 'imperial' series of special military postage stamps issued by Italy during the Second World War. They are surcharged P.M. (military post).

46 The collection of postmarks has recently become a marked trend among collectors. The examples include two French obliterations, one from the United States and one from the German Federal Republic.

47 A Channel Islands local stamp, produced in Guernsey by the Commodore Shipping line for communication with the neighbouring island of Sark.

48 An example of private post in Germany, issued in Hamburg towards the end of the nineteenth century by the Lafrenz company. Private companies in Germany were authorised to produce their own stamps in return for guaranteeing the percentage required by the Treasury.

49 Switzerland has always been noted for the excellent workmanship and the attention paid to detail in its stamps. This example, issued 1949, is remarkable for the softness of the engraving and the beauty and clarity of the design.

47

48

49

51

52

50-51-52
Photographic enlargement emphasises the artistic qualities of these three stamps. The first (top left) could be taken for a tapestry, and is a detail from an Austrian stamp issued in 1916. The other examples are Chinese, one bearing the Imperial dragon (issued 1897) and the other commemorating the anniversary of the reign of Emperor Hsuan T'ung (1909).

53 Errors can and do occur in stamp production, but it is not so much flaws in colour, typography and perforation that make imperfect stamps valuable; rather it is errors in design. This series was issued in 1961 to commemorate the Italian president's visit to Latin America. The bottom stamp contains a design error, which becomes glaringly apparent when it is compared with the one above: the contour of Peru is incorrect. The stamp was withdrawn at once, and is now highly valued.

54 The vicissitudes of political life are often reflected in postage stamps. These essays for a Mexico series bear the head of Maximilian, but before the stamps could be issued he was overthrown and put to death (1867).

53

54

55

55 A set of famous French 'Sower' stamps, renowned for the draughtsman's error in portraying the figure scattering grain against the wind, as indicated by the swirl of her skirt. In spite of the mistake the series was distributed for over 35 years (1903–38). It was even reissued between 1958–60. Moreover, this same stamp was used for the first two French surcharge issues. The 10 centimes, red, illustrated, is surcharged 5 centimes for the benefit of the Red Cross Organisation.

56 57

56 An example of a printing flaw in a strip of Italian stamps (1945) showing inking failure.

57 Three examples of misprints and defacements: a single stamp lacking perforation; a strip of three with an uninked fold; a strip of five imperforate at the top.

58 An Italian stamp with the numeral inverted.

59 Two Swiss examples of *tête-bêche* pairs, produced for books of stamps.

60 Former German states frequently printed square stamps in groups of four, for greater customer convenience. They could either be used as a quadruplet or separated into singles. A similar procedure has been employed more recently, by Spain.

61 An example of a 'set-off' on stamps. The overprint has transferred to the gummed back of the stamps when sheets were stacked on top of one another before the ink was dry.

SEGNATASSE
CENTESIMI

8

HELVETIA
5
HELVETIA
10

9

¼ FREIMARKE ¼
MECKLENB.
SCHWERIN
¼ SCHILLING ¼

0

OGLIO DI CENTO FRANC
REPUBBLICA
SOCIALE
ITALIANA
POSTE ITALIANE
25

61

62

63

62 It is common for stamps to be reprinted over a number of years, and when this happens variations in colour may appear. These two blocks of Italians (the first issued in 1930) show how significant the variation can be.

63 Special six-sided Belgian telegraph stamps, issued 1897–99.

64 65

64 Stamps have always varied considerably in size. A 'normal-sized' Italian is contrasted with two extremes: the British halfpenny, rose carmine, 1870, and the US newspaper stamp, 1865.

65 Extraordinarily vivid stamps from the island of Tonga, 1963. They show reproductions of current coinage printed on a special metallic paper.

66

67

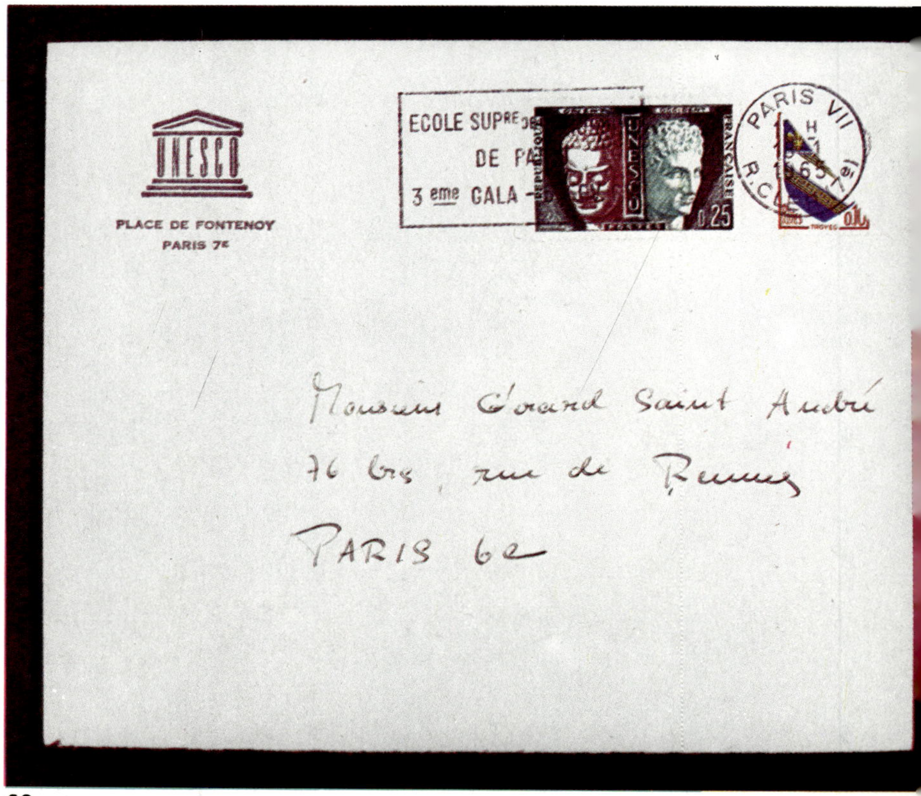

68

66 A very unusual example of an undelivered letter returned to the sender, a member of the French Assembly. The word 'TAXE' has been blocked out of the smaller stamp, a postage-due stamp, thereby validating it for regular use.

67 A group of four Italian tax stamps, overprinted to validate them for postage.

68 A 10 centimes stamp has been cut diagonally in half on this Unesco letter, to meet a shortage of the 5 centimes denomination.

69 70

69 Three examples of local post office obliterations by hand, in default of an official cancellation frank. A hand-written note across the bottom three stamps explains that the official obliterator at Cavriago was broken at the time, 22 August 1865.

70 The front and back of an envelope sent from Egypt to Morocco and subject to additional taxation in Morocco (the surcharge indicated by the 'T' in the triangles).

71

71 A group of special wartime stamps issued in Italy during the Nazi occupation. A private company, Corrieri Alta Italia, was authorised to deliver mail by bicycle or motorcycle between Turin and Venice, because of the breakdown of the rail system.

72 An example of double stamping during the German occupation of the Channel Islands. This envelope has a conventional Jersey stamp as well as a 25 pfenning German issue, with the head of Adolf Hitler. The franking marks indicate that it has been delivered by military mail.

72

73

74

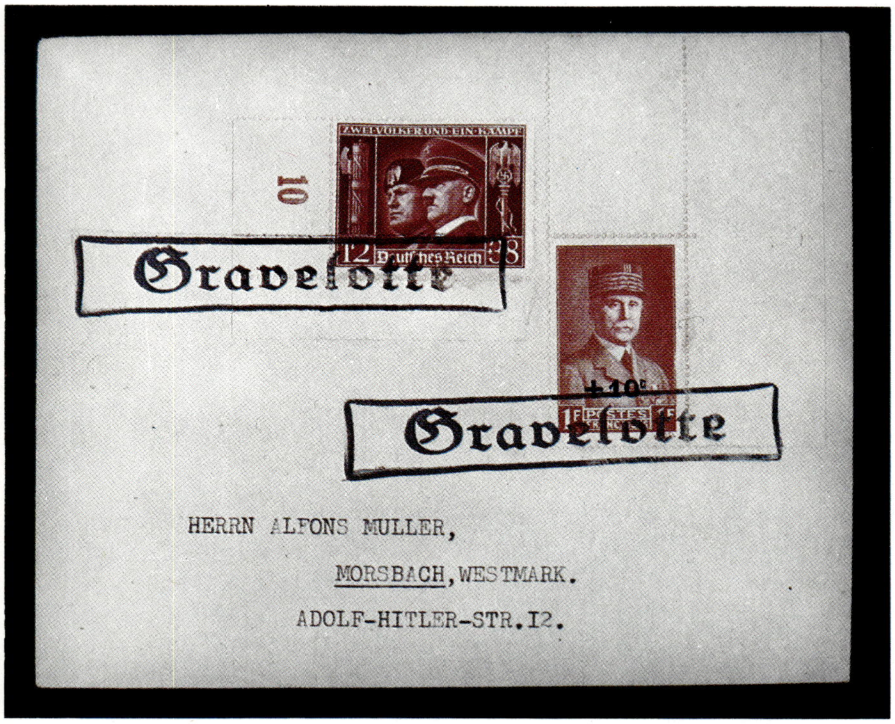

73 Another example of multiple stamping during the German occupation of Lorraine. A German stamp with the head of former President Hindenburg accompanies two French stamps.

74 This letter, sent from Lorraine during the Nazi occupation, carries a German stamp bearing the heads of both Hitler and Mussolini, as well as a French stamp bearing a portrait of Pétain. Since the French stamp had no validity in occupied territory, its inclusion must have been meant as a gesture of solidarity with the Vichy régime and the Nazis.

75 A series of Italian stamps overprinted for use in Trieste and Trentino, disputed territories over which Italy claimed jurisdiction at the end of the First World War.

75

76

76 Fiume was one of many territories whose possession was bitterly disputed at the end of the First World War. It was taken from Hungary, existed temporarily as a free state (following D'Annunzio's brief reign of glory) and was finally annexed by Italy in 1924. These stamps and overprints provide what is virtually an encapsulated history.

77

78

77 The economic crisis in Germany after the First World War was reflected in the current postage stamps. Runaway inflation rendered the mark increasingly valueless, so that everyday stamps were issued in fantastically high denominations.

78 German inflation reached its peak in 1923, by which time even the unit 'million' had been discarded.

79

80
81

79 Few philatelists were aware, at the time, that following the Russian Revolution in 1917, stamps commemorating the tercentenary of the Romanov dynasty were superscribed with the insignia of the French Revolution, a Phrygian cap, crossed swords and the motto, 'Liberty, Equality, Fraternity'.

80 A letter carrying stamps of the former Austro-Hungary Empire, overprinted following the creation of the new Czechoslovak Republic.

81 A French military postcard issued in Poland, November 1919.

82
83

82 A set of special stamps issued in Schleswig-Holstein after the First World War, when the inhabitants of the area were given the chance of deciding by plebiscite whether to join Denmark or Germany.

83 The overprinting on this group of Bavarian stamps, following Germany's defeat in 1918, marked the end of Bavaria's postal (and political) autonomy.

84 An example of franking used in Italy in 1944, when there was a dire shortage of postage stamps. The frank 'R.P.' indicates the payment of postal dues.

85 An enlarged fragment of a stamp issued by Czechoslovakia (1919–20), for use by the Czechoslovak Legion serving in Siberia.

86 The post-war shortage of stamps in Madagascar led to the use of a special marking, indicating payment of postage.

84

85

Par Avion

CARTE POSTALE.

Nom et adresse de l'éditeur :

GOLAZ FILS

Case Postale 92

Carte vendue 0 fr. 10 dans tous les bureaux de Poste.

MADAGASCAR ET DÉPENDANCES

POSTE AÉRIENNE—TAMATAVE

Taxe perçue 10 Fr. 90 c.

Messieurs,
Au moment où la France peut être considérée comme libérée, nous saisissons le premier courrier pour venir prendre de vos nouvelles. Nous serions heureux d'apprendre que la tourmente vous a épargnés dans vos personnes, vos affections et vos biens et que vous avez pu maintenir votre activité. - Nous n'ignorons pas que, du fait de la guerre, il y a tout un plan de reconstruction à réaliser et, par priorité, d'immenses besoins à satisfaire en Europe avant d'envisager l'importation vers les Colonies.

Messieurs LAPORTE,
BISQUIT & C°
JARNAC-COGNAC

TAMATAVE 6 OCT 44 JOURNAUX P.P.

87 These Italian stamps have been overprinted during the Nazi occupation of Zara. The Germans had dislodged Italian forces loyal to Mussolini's successor, who was attempting to negotiate a separate peace with the Allies.

88 Another example of Nazi overprinting during the brief occupation of Zara.

89 The tiny Commune of Campione, an Italian enclave in Switzerland, successfully avoided occupation in 1944 and remained faithful to the Italian monarchy. But it issued its own stamps, valued in Swiss francs.

90 War brings censorship in its wake, as these envelopes clearly demonstrate. The frankings indicate the date on which the letter has been opened and read, and the date on which it has been returned to the post.

CENT. 50
Deutsche Besetzung Zara
POSTE ITALIANE
Deutsche Besetzung Zara
TUTTO E TUTTI PER LA VITTORIA
Deutsche Besetzung Zara
POSTE ITALIANE CENT. 35
Deutsche Besetzung Zara
AUGUSTUS IMPERATOR
LIRE POSTE ITALIANE 1,75

87

CARTOLINA POSTALE
OPERE DEL REGIME - ROMA
CASE DEI MUTILATI
CARTOLINA POSTALE
CARTOLINA POSTALE
CARTOLINA POSTALE
PONTE DEL LITTORIO

88

RR. POSTE ITALIANE
1 Fr.
COMUNE DI CAMPIONE
COURVOISIER S. A.

89

COMMISSIONE PROV. CENSURA
47 R
Verificato
LEVA O PER LA IL GIORNO
17 SET 1943
RESTITUITA ALLE POSTE PER INOLTRO IL GIORNO
17 SET 1942
VERIFICATO
Signori
Fratelli Olivari

90

91

92

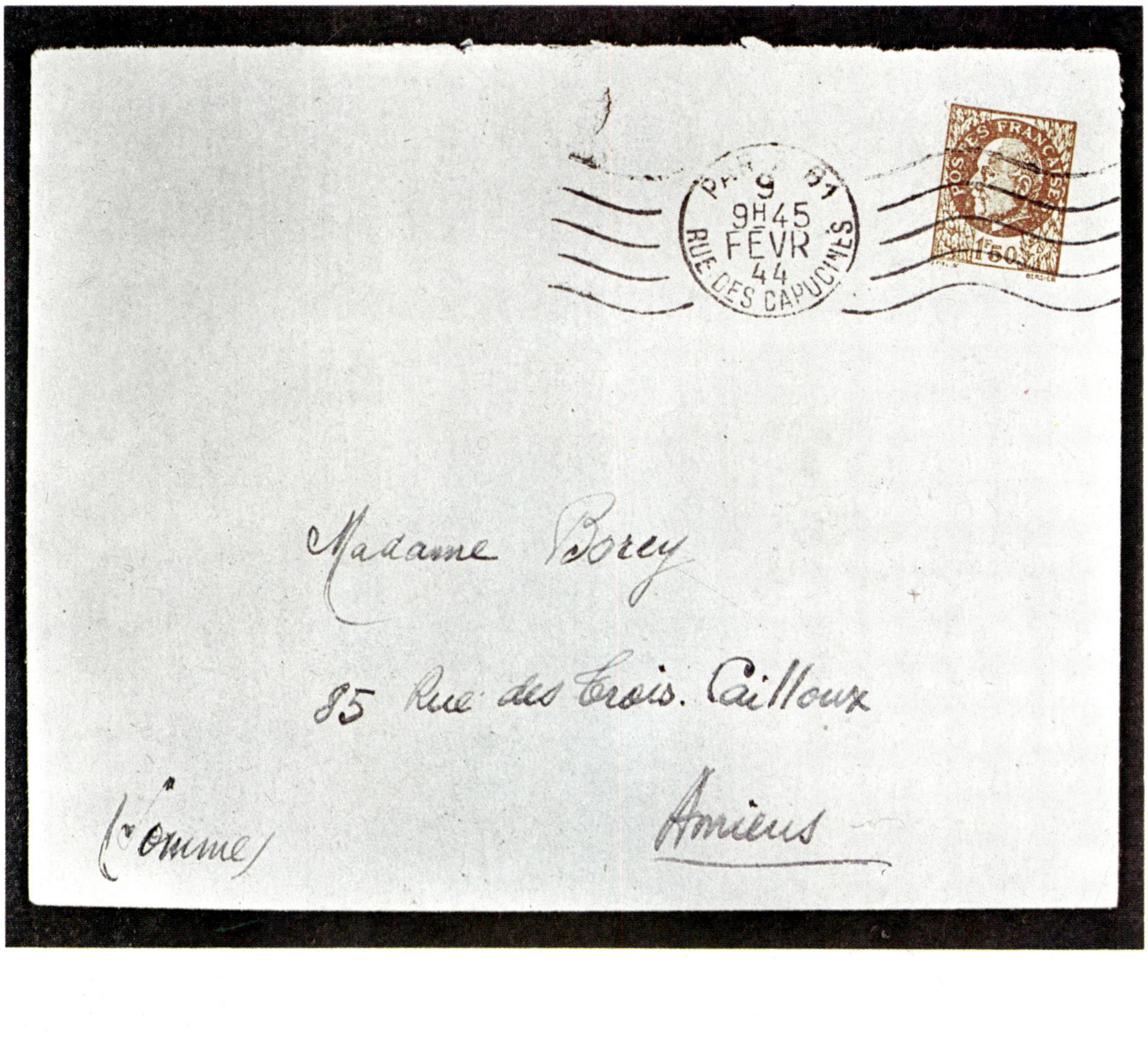

91 First-day cover marking the inauguration of the new postal service in Naples, during the Anglo-American occupation.

92 During the war the Intelligence Service forged stamps for use by its agents in France and Germany (stamps bearing Pétain's and Hitler's effigies respectively). This enabled the agents to mail out tracts to the people – at the expense of the Nazi and Vichy governments. The French Resistance also produced forged stamps to defraud the Vichy postal service. Envelopes bearing such forged stamps are rare.

93 At the end of the war, many unofficial stamps were issued to commemorate Resistance fighters. This is a souvenir sheet brought out in Italy in 1945.

94 A selection of stamps issued in post-war Germany by the occupying powers.

FOGLIETTO-RICORDO - FEUILLET-SOUVENIR
S. A. C. P. I. - Servizio Alpino Collegamento Postale Interinale - Alta Dumentina
"La Stella-Alpina è una delle doti dell'Alta Dumentina,, Emissione Locale "Serie Floreale,, 1945
FRANCOBOLLO "CARTOLINA" S. A. C. P. I. ALTA DUMENTINA L. 0.50
FRANCOBOLLO "LETTERA" S. A. C. P. I. ALTA DUMENTINA L. 1
FRANCOBOLLO RECAPITO "EXPRES" L. 15 L. 15 ALTA DUMENTINA S.A.C.P.I.
Francobollo "Raccomandata" S. A. C. P. I. ALTA DUMENTINA L. 1.50
FRANCOBOLLO "Estero-Etranger" SACPI L. 2 ALTA DUMENTINA

93
94

DEUTSCHE 1 PFENNIG POST
DEUTSCHE 5 PFENNIG POST
DEUTSCHE 1 RM POST
DEUTSCHE 8 PFENNIG POST
DEUTSCHE 20 PFENNIG POST
3 AM POST 3 PFENNIG DEUTSCHLAND
5 AM POST 5 PFENNIG DEUTSCHLAND
8 AM POST 8 PFENNIG DEUTSCHLAND
12 AM POST 12 PFENNIG DEUTSCHLAND
15 AM POST 15 PFENNIG DEUTSCHLAND
ZONE FRANCAISE 1F BRIEFPOST 1F
ZONE FRANCAISE 20F BRIEFPOST 20F
NOTOPFER 2 BERLIN STEUERMARKE
40 PFENNIG Sowjetische Besatzungs Zone DEUTSCHE POST
ZONE FRANCAISE 15F BRIEFPOST 15F
ZONE FRANCAISE 12F BRIEFPOST 12F

95

96

97

95 United Nations stamps, inscribed in English, French, Spanish and Russian.

96 Pope Pius XI authorised the issue of these special stamps, following the concordat with Italy in 1929 which established the independent status of the Vatican.

97 Three sets of Italian stamps issued in different years in support of European unity.

98 The first Greek stamps, issued in 1861, bore the head of the god Mercury.

99 Between the death of one pope and the election of his successor, the pontifical emblem appears below the words *SEDE VACANTE* (seat vacant). These stamps were issued in 1963, following the death of Pope John XXIII.

100 In 1919 Danzig became a free state, and remained so between the wars. The top stamp, issued in 1920, is German with a Danzig overprint. Below are several stamps issued by Danzig in the following years, and at the bottom, a Polish stamp overprinted 'PORT GDANSK' (Gdansk is the Polish name for Danzig).

98

99

100

101 102

101 This stamp represents the great Spanish knight El Cid, who was renowned above all for his campaigns against the Moorish power in Spain. The irony of it is, the stamp was issued by General Franco during the Spanish Civil War, at a time when he was employing Moroccan mercenaries in his campaign to overthrow the government of the Spanish Republic.

102 The first commemorative stamp issued by France (1923), in memory of the scientific achievements of the distinguished biologist, Louis Pasteur.

103 A set of Belgian charity stamps, each bearing a premium to aid tuberculosis research.

103

104

105

104 British colonies provide one of the richest fields for specialising. Those illustrated are stamps for Gibraltar, from the time of Queen Victoria to the modern day.

105 Nearly every nation in the Americas has issued stamps commemorating Christopher Columbus. This is a beautiful example from Chile (1867).

106

107

108

106 Swiss stamps displaying national legends and emblems: William Tell (centre), his son with the apple and crossbow, and Helvetia with the white cross of Switzerland on her breast.

107 A 1962 United States commemorative, issued after Colonel John Glenn became the first American in space.

108 The annual Swiss series, *Pro Juventute* (for young people), is eagerly sought by collectors because of the variety and interest of the subject matter.

109 A Swiss pair commemorating the Winter Olympics, held at St Moritz in 1948.

110 A stamp issued by the People's Republic of China, proclaiming solidarity with the revolutionary struggles in Africa.

111 Examples of the Michelangelo series, issued in Italy (1961).

112 113

112 These Italian commemoratives are really stamps within stamps. They were issued to mark the centenaries of the first stamps issued by the Italian states (plate 17).

113 An exceptionally detailed German commemorative (1943) representing an old-fashioned courier mail diligence, with the post-horn insignia on the outside of the carriage door.

114

114 Italian commemoratives honouring early postal services, the first representing a mail diligence and the second the famous Sardinian *Cavallini* (plate 4).

115 A selection of commemoratives honouring famous Italians, and stirring episodes in Italian history.

115

116

116 A set of four French commemoratives honouring outstanding pioneers in the field of medicine.

117 A commemorative issued by Monaco in 1955 in honour of the great French writer of science fiction, Jules Verne.

118 Monaco has issued many stamps on religious themes, in this case a tribute to St Bernadette of Lourdes.

119 A French tribute to book publishing and the art of book binding.

117

118

119

120

121

120 Austria paid tribute to some of the greatest musicians in a set of seven commemoratives issued in 1922. These stamps were sold at a price ten times their face value, to raise money for impoverished musicians.

121 A portrait of the composer Franz Liszt, an exceptionally beautiful Austrian commemorative issue (1961) marking the 150th anniversary of his birth.

122 123

124 125

126

122 Four commemoratives, one from Gabon and three from Poland, on the theme of space exploration.

123 A good example of the use of stamps for educational as well as postal purposes.

124 A classic issue from French West Africa.

125 A postcard from the German Empire, used by civil servants during the First World War. It is interesting to note the 10 centimes surcharge, which validates it for use in France.

126 An Israeli commemorative envelope, issued for the Boy Scout Jamboree in 1956.

127

128

129

127 Two blocks of four Italian stamps specially overprinted for the Venice National Congress of Philately, September 1945.

128 Imperforate North Korean stamps, commemorating events and heroes of the Korean War.

129 A commemorative miniature sheet in honour of the International Philately Exhibition at Milan. Each stamp is perforated with an initial representing the event.

130

131

130 Several examples of stamps issued in connection with the International Red Cross Organisation.

131 A French commemorative paying tribute to blood donors.

132 Early commemoratives: two interesting examples marking the 25th anniversary of the reign of the Prince Regent, Leopold of Bavaria.

133 A French tribute to polio vaccine.

132 133

134

135

134 Deeply-rooted cultural traditions are reflected in this issue from Saudi Arabia (1922), reminiscent of the design of an Oriental carpet.

135 Examples of an exceptionally beautiful Belgium series, issued in connection with the reconstruction of the Abbey of Orval, 1941–2.

136 Stamps issued by smaller nations are frequently among the most beautiful: this reproduction of 'Virgin and Child', by Luca della Robbia, was issued by Ireland for the Marian Year, 1953–4.

137 A set of four airmail stamps on a musical theme, issued by Laos in 1953.

136

137

138

139

138 The artistic talents of the Greek people have been expressed in her postage stamps. The treasures of Crete are represented in this superb series of multicoloured stamps issued in 1951. The stamp in the centre commemorates the 1000th anniversary of the liberation of Crete.

139 This beautiful multicoloured series was issued in 1963 to commemorate the celebrated empresses of Ethiopia, from the Queen of Sheba to the wife of the Emperor Menelik II.

140

141

142

140 Five examples of the recent US series commemorating American artists.

141 In 1961 the principality of Monaco issued a series of rare beauty, illustrating the history of the automobile. The four cars shown here portray some of the most celebrated cars of the past.

142 A series of Dutch stamps, portraying regional headdresses, which were issued in support of children's charities.

143

144

144 One of the most beautiful series on an artistic theme is that issued by Belgium in 1941. This example represents a statue of St Martin dividing his cloak.

143 Japan has issued for some years an annual series to mark 'philately week'. These beautifully designed and printed stamps reproduce famous works of art as well as national costumes.

145 Philatelists engaged in thematic collecting are unlikely to ignore this splendid series of elephant stamps, issued by Laos in 1958.

145

146

148

147

146 A set of religious stamps issued by Spain in 1954, in connection with the Marian Year.

147 In 1956 Spain issued these two special stamps marking the 75th anniversary of the crowning of the Black Virgin of Montserrat.

148 Switzerland has paid particular attention to stamps representing the countryside. The top example was issued in 1942 for the National Day celebrations and the second millennium of Geneva; the one below was issued in 1944, also on the occasion of the National Day celebrations, and represents the village of St Jacob.

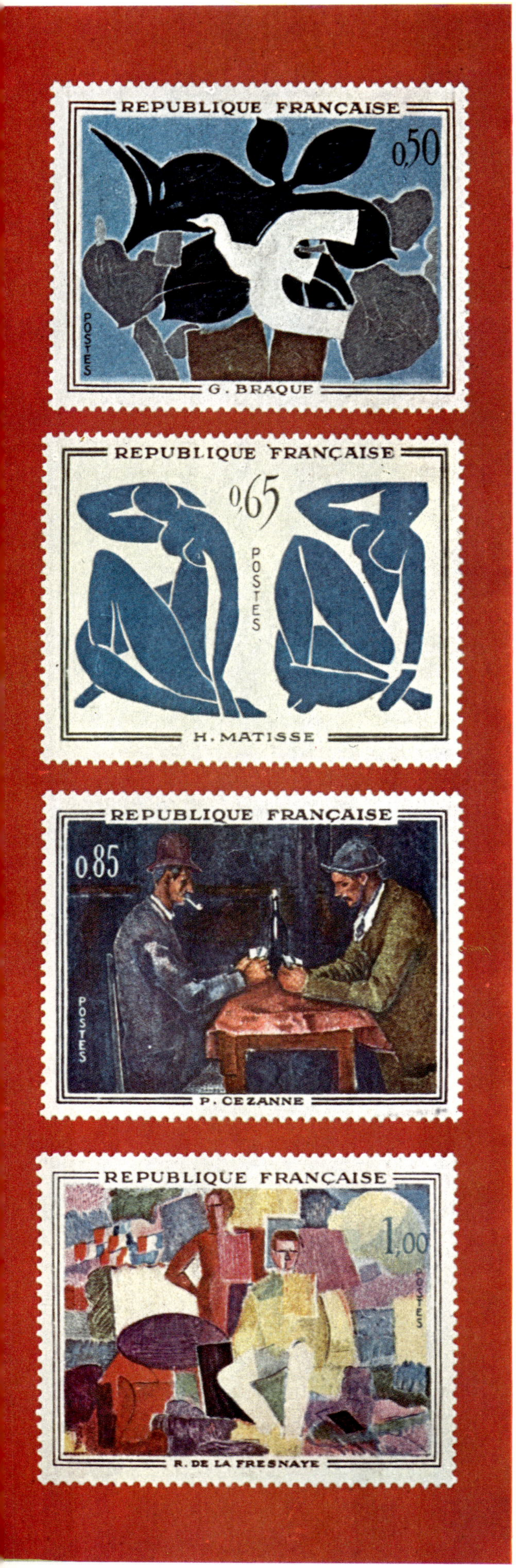

149

150

149 In 1961 France issued an exceptionally beautiful, multicoloured set of four values devoted to modern art.

150 A floral series issued by the Dutch Antilles in 1955, in aid of children's charities.

151 152

151 Alpine flowers are represented in these stamps from an Austrian series of 1948.

152 The beauty of this recent Austrian series has been admired by non-collectors as well as collectors.

153

153 Flowers and butterflies: splendid examples of the Swiss *Pro Juventute* series.

154 Two examples of a set of five Czechoslovak stamps, issued in 1956 and featuring different types of fungi.

155 In 1961 Czechoslovakia issued stamps portraying butterflies. These two examples illustrate the freshness of the design.

156 In 1955 France issued a series representing the fauna of her Southern and Antarctic territories.

154

ČESKOSLOVENSKO
60h
Kozák křemenáč
Krombholzia rufesc.
K. SVOLINSKÝ · L. JIRKA
ČESKOSLOVENSKO
40h
Boletus edulis
Hřib borovák
K. SVOLINSKÝ · JIRKA

ČESKOSLOVENSKO
30 h
PARNASSIUS APOLLO L.
JASOŇ ČERVENOOKÝ
M. ŠVABINSKÝ PINX.
JINDRA S. SC.
ČESKOSLOVENSKO
60 h
NYMPHALIS JO L.
BABOČKA PAVÍ OKO
M. ŠVABINSKÝ PINX.
JINDRA S. SC.

155

TERRES AUSTRALES ET ANTARCTIQUES FRANÇAISES
RF
POSTES
8F
ILES ST-PAUL ET DE LA NOUVELLE AMSTERDAM
TERRES AUSTRALES ET ANTARCTIQUES FRANÇAISES
RF
POSTES
5F
ILES ST-PAUL ET DE LA NOUVELLE AMSTERDAM
TERRES AUSTRALES ET ANTARCTIQUES FRANÇAISES
POSTES
10F
ARCHIPEL DES KERGUELEN
RF
TERRES AUSTRALES ET ANTARCTIQUES FRANÇAISES
POSTES
RF
1F
ARCHIPEL des CROZET
TERRES AUSTRALES ET ANTARCTIQUES FRANÇAISES
POSTES
15F
ARCHIPEL DES KERGUELEN
RF
TERRES AUSTRALES ET ANTARCTIQUES FRANÇAISES
POSTES
RF
ARCHIPEL des CROZET
0F50

156

157

158

159

160

161

157 Three of the most celebrated Mediterranean beauty spots are represented in these stamps, from a post-war French series.

158 This beautifully designed and engraved French stamp, issued in 1954, shows a street scene in Quimper.

159 Lourdes is represented in the same French series of 1954. The stamp is particularly prized by collectors if it is on an envelope, and has been obliterated in the town itself.

160 A bi-coloured reproduction of the famous bridge at Valentré de Cahors, issued in the French tourist series of 1955.

161 An Austrian stamp issued in 1960, on the occasion of the 40th anniversary of the plebiscite in Carinthia, held after the First World War. Both Austria and Yugoslavia laid claim to the territory, but the plebiscite went in Austria's favour.

162 Exhibits from the Museum of Communications are illustrated in this 1959 Hungarian series on transportation.

163 Propaganda stamps issued by Nazi Germany during the Second World War. A first set of twelve values was issued in 1943, followed by a similar set the next year.

164 Many stamps are issued both perforate and imperforate. This example from the USSR celebrates the space flight of Lunik IV, in 1963.

162

163

164

165

166

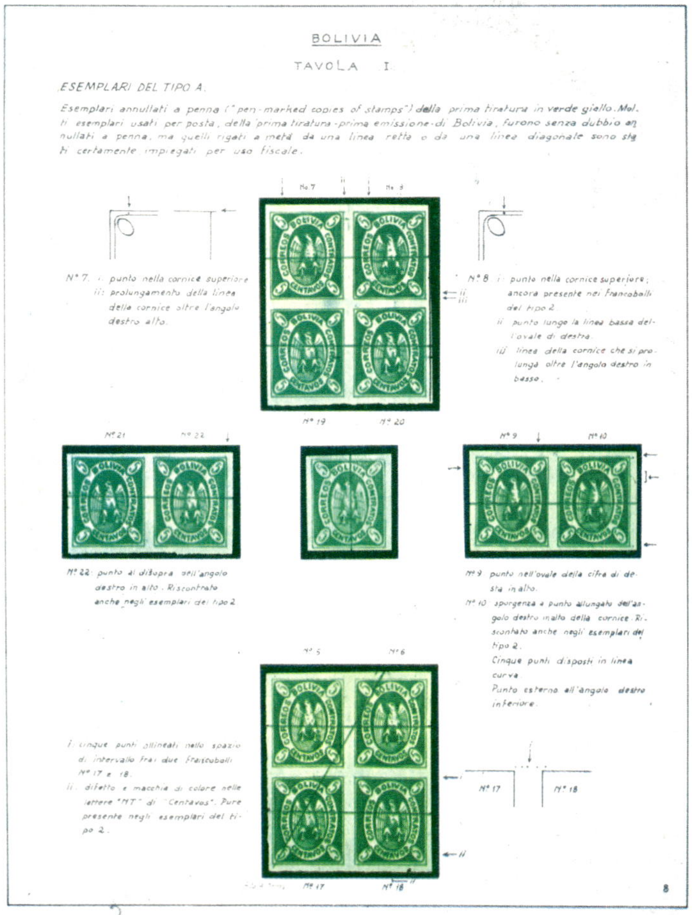

dalla Collezione Sant'Uberto

167

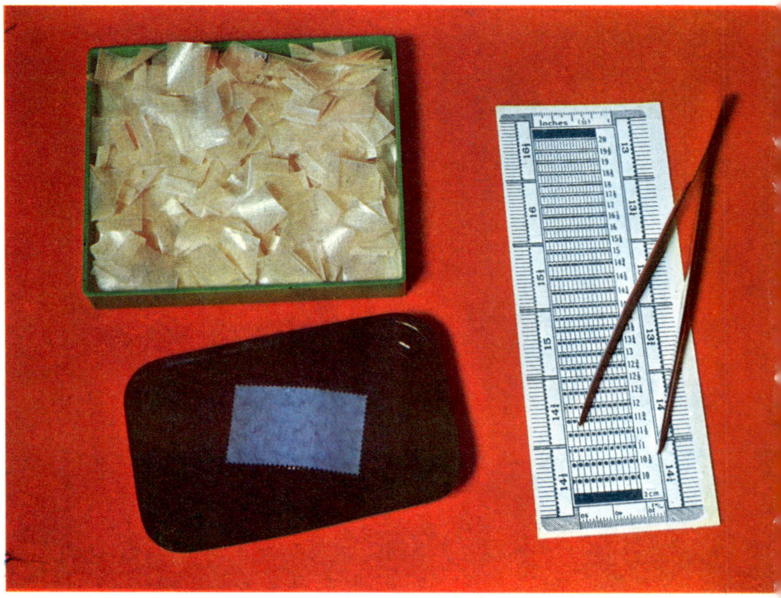

165 A genuine gold 'stamp': famous and rare postage stamps can be reproduced as medallions.

166 A page from a modern stamp collection using the stock-book method. The stamps are firmly held in position by means of long strips of transparent plastic, thereby obviating the need for stamp hinges.

167 Highly sophisticated collections really become books on the history, the technique and the art of the postage stamp. The page illustrated concerns only one Bolivian stamp, its errors, printing differences and so forth, all carefully annotated.

168 Useful, almost essential equipment for any collector: stamp hinges, perforation gauge, tweezers and a watermark tray (used with benzine).